Stupid Ways, Smart Ways to Think About
GOD

Stupid Ways, Smart Ways to Think About GOD

Michael Shevack
and
Jack Bemporad

Triumph™ Books
Liguori, Missouri

Published by Triumph™ Books
Liguori, Missouri
An imprint of Liguori Publications

Library of Congress Cataloging-in-Publication Data

Shevack, Michael.
    Stupid ways, smart ways to think about God / Michael
Shevack and Jack Bemporad
      p. cm.
      ISBN 0-89243-577-1 : $13.95
      1. God — Popular works.   I. Bemporad, Jack.   II. Title.
    BT 102.S495   1993
    231 — dc20   93-12905
                                                         CIP

To Trish and Alex, for enduring.
And in loving memory of
Aaron Sherman and Alan Rosenberg.

Contents

Stupid Ways, Smart Ways to Think About

GOD

Introduction

Somewhere in the heart of each of us sits an old man with snow-white hair and a long, flowing beard. He lives in a beautiful palace of light, way up in the sky. Clouds, like taxicabs, carry visitors to and fro. Winged angels flutter about, harp music playing in the background like celestial Muzak.

This divinely enthroned man, looking suspiciously like a transfigured Charlton Heston, is God. God the first time most of us become acquainted with Him.*

This was God the King. Benevolent Monarch of the World. He was kind and loving, like Mommy. Trustworthy, but firm, like Daddy. Wise and patient like Grandpa. He was the perfect picture of God for a child who was too innocent to envision anything else.

---

* Had the English language a decent third-person, neuter pronoun it would have been very helpful. Alas, for the purposes of this book, God will be referred to as "He." Reluctantly. And, of course, stupidly.

He was a good God. That is, until we grew up. Until we traded our childhood fantasies for real life. Until we needed to wrest control of our lives and didn't want interference from our parents or an overly parental God.

He was a real God. That is, until mankind grew up, began to trade mythology for scientific theory, learned to prize logic over feeling, and discovered so much about the world that this God seemed stupid.

The old man in the sky became less than believable after mankind peered through a telescope. The kingly god became undesirable after the revolutionary concept of democracy. And the beard was hardly politically correct after women's liberation.

In many ways, we've grown smarter. But when it comes to God, many of use haven't grown at all. We know what's "wrong" with God, but not what's "right." We haven't really thought through, openly and completely, this idea of one singular, supreme Being. We have not come to terms with our view of God in light of everything we now know and feel about the world.

We still have stupid ways of thinking about God. *Stupid*, from the Latin, meaning "stop." Our ideas about God have simply stopped growing, stopped maturing, stopped developing, and now seem stupid even in the commonplace meaning of the word.

The ideas we were spoon-fed as children we now gag on as adults. The ideas that fired our imagination and inspired our reverence now seem laughable. God seems like little more than a human invention so cluttered with absurdities that he's barely recognizable.

Even the truest believers have been plagued by doubts. Real doubts. Healthy doubts. Doubts that come from trying to approach God as whole people. Doubts that come from trying to reconcile their intelligence and their sense of reason with what they learned in Sunday school.

For others, there has been no struggle. God has simply become too unbelievable to believe. But if you talk to these atheists and ask them *why* they can't believe, you very quickly see the real problem.

Atheists seldom reject God — a credible God, that is. More often, they reject some stupid way of thinking about God. Some idea so ridiculous it isn't worth believing. Some idea that causes so much personal guilt it is better off discarded. And rightly so.

For them, and indeed for all of us, the question is not if there is, or could be, a God, but what *kind* of god is God? What sort of God do we believe in? What kind of God is *worthy* of belief? Often we've pushed aside our confusion. In an attempt to feel whole, we've brushed it under a rug, written it off as "mystery."

Most of the time we can get away with it, and our stupid ways of thinking go unnoticed. But many times we are confronted quite abruptly by our stupid ways of thinking. There is a senseless death; then the idea that God is perfectly good seems senseless. A woman is raped; then the stupid idea that God is male becomes poison. Divorce becomes a necessity; then a lifetime of faith is thrown into jeopardy. Indeed, "life crisis" and "faith crisis" always seem to go hand in hand.

Why, however, do we question the *existence of God* at these moments? Shouldn't we instead question our stupid ways of thinking about Him? Is the problem God? Or are we the problem? Maybe what we really need is a smart way to think about God. Some idea less fragile, less silly, more complete. Some idea that's strong enough to withstand reality, because it's flexible enough to grow as we need to grow.

But where do we find one?

Religions contain many wonderful ways to think about God. But all too often these wonderful ways are so buried under a morass of superstition that it's hard to find what we're looking for. Original meanings have been blurred by mistranslation and misinterpretation. The significance of rituals has been lost. Ideas that once served crucial social and political functions are now irrelevant.

Religions, too, have often made the task of finding a smart way to think about God more difficult. In an attempt to insulate their traditions, they've often made human inquiry a sin. Intelligent questions are frequently greeted with suspicion.

In an age in which science has stolen the stage from religion, where only the truths gleaned from controlled experiments are valid, where only the practical, material results are valued, any search for God is denigrated as a remnant of more primitive times. Indeed, a smart way to think about God is perceived as a contradiction in terms.

So what's a searcher to do?

These days, this question is more important than ever. The baby boomers have grown up. They're booming with babies of their own. They're searching for meaning, trying to give their children a sense of values. Religious affiliation is soaring. Church and synagogue attendance is reaching an all-time high.

People who left their faith in rebellion are returning in droves. They will be forced, once again, to confront some of the stupid ways of thinking that drove them away to begin with. They will be put in the precarious situation of having to teach them to their children.

More than ever, we need smart ways to think about God. Ways that are worth passing on to a new generation. The purpose of this book is to help you find them.

Certainly, we can't provide all answers for all people. But we can begin to clear some of the cobwebs. We can begin to strip away, one at a time, some of the stupid ways of thinking about God that have caused so many problems. We can "separate the wheat from the chaff" and take a fresh look at God. And, we hope to leave you with at least one way of thinking about God that is smart.

People do not like to have their beliefs challenged. No doubt, for many, the process will be downright painful. So we hope a little touch of humor will be appreciated. Especially for a subject that has become a little too serious.

Nevertheless, if we can get your head nodding, get you rethinking how you think about God, inspire you to grow, seek and find, we will have succeeded.

We all, each and every one of us, start out with a stupid way of thinking about God. Materialistic people see materialistic gods. Egotistical people see egotistical gods. Militaristic people see militaristic gods. Macho people see macho gods.

But, with a little effort, and a lot of honesty, we can see through these stupid ways of thinking. See through them and let them go.

Then smart ways of thinking about God may not be far behind.

Will the real God please stand up?

Stupid Ways
to Think About
GOD

...and I'd like a wake up call at 10:00

Stupid Way 1
God the Cosmic Bellhop

od, I'm checking in. Though just for a short stay. But while I'm here, please see to it I have a wide-screen color TV. Make that a Sony. A new Porsche convertible. Red, of course. And, oops, I almost forgot. A large Dr Pepper. Heavy on the ice. AMEN."

Welcome to the Heaven Hilton. God, the ever-gracious Host, ready to serve you. The accommodations are perfect. Truly everything you want. But that's the problem.

Just ring the bell, and God becomes your own personal Pavlovian puppy. Eagerly He goes to work, gratifying your every desire, indulging your every whim.

Yes, this is a god who will help you meet the mortgage. A god who intercedes with the boss on your behalf.

We pray to him when we're overextended. We praise him when our lottery ticket wins.

We expect him to respond to all our petitions as automatically as a 24-hour cash machine. To reorder the cosmos in order to cater to our needs.

Now, could anything be more stupid? Yet how often, in our attempt to cope with life, we take the noble notion of the Universal, Objective, Justice-seeking Deity — a God who is supposed to be served by us — and turn Him into a manservant.

Despite our lip service, despite our respectable intonations and self-effacement, we cannot disguise the truth: We believe we can simply order God what to do. We are living the stupid idea that God's sole purpose is to underwrite our ego, our selfishness. That God is the way, not to greater expansion, nor to peace with oneself and one's fellowman, but to the ignoble gratification of our own petty desires.

When we think of God as a Cosmic Bellhop, we show how strongly we cling to our infantile desires to control and manipulate those around us. We also show a lack of faith in our ability to provide for ourselves.

But God forbid, you stiff Him on tips, and He doesn't place the entire universe at your feet. What do you do?

You double-lock the door to your suite. Hang up a Do Not Disturb sign. Refuse all calls.

You act like an angry child. And continue this self-indulgence to its ultimate form: You cease to believe.

Herein lies the challenge: Do you recognize that the concept of God you have been using is inadequate? Do you realize that you have created it? Do you understand that you have set up unrealistic expectations for God and doomed your faith from the start?

It is not unreasonable to expect a god who is concerned about our welfare to be responsive to our needs.

But it is unreasonable to expect God to provide us with magic. To grant all our wishes at the sound of a bell.

And it is preposterous to expect there is no protocol, no proper moral attitude that is minimally required to elicit His response.

But the question is: Are you willing to explore other approaches that can make God more accessible? Ways that work better in the real world?

In short, do you choose to grow? Or do you choose, out of a naive self-centeredness, to remain stupid?

For truly, a belief in God as Cosmic Bellhop is something that sooner or later will prove itself shortsighted. Such a view cannot correspond to the complexity of life as most of us experience it. After all, you have created a Designer God. A God that fits you, and only you, perfectly.

And, by making God an extension of your own desires, you have made your own desires God-like. In essence, you have made yourself God. You are the center of the universe and God is at the periphery.

That hardly resembles a healthy faith. Indeed, it is more akin to cult behavior. It turns man into God. It has a very ancient name, *idolatry*. Because the first step in any meaningful religion is to recognize our proper place in the scheme of things.

But when you make God your Cosmic Bellhop, it's you who ends up carrying the baggage.

Stupid Way 2
God as Little Mary Sunshine

h, Eternally-smiling One. Thou art more friendly than Mister Rogers. More sunny than Doris Day. Thou art the best little god anyone could ever have.

Yes, put on your polarizers. It's time to bask in the glorious light of Little Mary Sunshine. Everyone's favorite kind of god. And why not?

He's a hap-hap-happy deity. Hovering over you like an umbrella on a rainy day.

You've got problems? Why worry? Why work at life? Little Mary Sunshine will take care of everything for you. Just relax. Catch some rays. But be careful. Prolonged exposure can be harmful.

For little Mary Sunshine is a god of illusions. A god devoid of substance.

This view of God masquerades as a simple, almost enviable, childlike faith. It may even resemble, in its purity, a standard worth aspiring to. But its resemblance, and everything about it, is superficial.

This god is all love. But not real love. He nourishes, but does not discipline. He coddles, but does not upbraid.

God has been homogenized of all dimension, pasteurized of all impurities, until he is bland and suitable for middle-class palates.

This "divine" love has been rendered so simplistic, so comfortable it is not real. It bears no relation to any of the complications we experience in life.

Indeed, Little Mary Sunshine shines so brightly we are blinded.

How could a God this good be responsible for a world filled with such suffering and cruelty? It's so hard to believe, many Mary Sunshine devotees deny the existence of evil whatsoever, when what they should deny is this concept of God.

Others explain evil by believing in demons, devils, Darth Vader, or some other character in a cosmic comic book of right vs. wrong. Suddenly, our all-powerful God has a competitor. Who's the real god anyway?

Yet, this is just a Pandora's box of theological Band-Aids. All to protect a god that is too good. A god that defies our God-given sense of reason, because he has created all light and no shadow. Something is missing.

This concept of God is not just intellectually unsatisfying. It is also emotionally crippling. Because Little Mary Sunshine is a god of fragile people, desperate people who need to escape the imperfections of life. And the darker sides of themselves.

This god we have created for ourselves is also a fragile god. He is decimated by wars. Abandoned after the senseless death of a child. His benevolence all too often feels like a lie. Yes, this is a god we have cursed.

But all our goddammits are also rays of hope, if we choose to see them as such. They compel us to face the stupidity of our belief system. They encourage us to create a concept of God that works in the real world. And a faith that is so all-embracing it even shines in the light of human reason.

Our disillusionment with this God is only natural, when we create an illusion to begin with. We set ourselves up for our ultimate disappointment.

Might there not be a way of thinking about God that is more durable? A god that is not the projection of the Pollyanna within us? A god who loves but is not impotent? Because we have allowed him to mature, at least to adolescence?

One thing is sure, all up and no down is not just a stupid way to see God. It is a drug. And a dangerous one.

Believe too much in Little Mary Sunshine, and you're bound to get burned.

Stupid Way 3
The Marquis de God

ANTED:
Dominant deity for submissive person. Must be into pain and bondage. Willing to inflict human suffering in pursuit of satisfaction. Humiliation techniques a plus. Sense of humor not required. Inquire P.O. Box G.O.D.

Get out the whips, the chains, the earthquakes, the pestilence. It's time for some good old-fashioned fun. With a good old-fashioned god.

Yes, this is the proverbial god of wrath. The Marquis de God. Ready to show you how much he cares by punishing you.

There's no end to the playful little tools in his pleasure arsenal. In a moment of rage, continents convulse with seismic activity. In a fit of moral indignation, he demonstrates the latest craze in viral mutations.

And his skill with floods is legendary.

But this is no game between consenting adults. This is a stupid way of thinking about God. Pure negativity that is positively destructive.

For the Marquis de God is simply a god who hates. This is a deity who despises sin and sinners with such passion that he'll murder in order to exterminate them.

He forces his noblest creation to dance like a trained poodle on the brink of annihilation. Grace, like a dog biscuit, offered or withdrawn, depending on performance.

If this is the only way you want to think about God, you have no other choice. You learn to like it. You learn to love it.

But let's play fair. The Marquis de God may be an old grouch. He may be cruel and despotic. But he does have a good side. He knows how to keep mankind humble. And let's face it, that's quite an accomplishment.

His acts of Holy Suppression, his Divine threats of Doom, help make us aware of our own helplessness. We become diminished in his presence, infantilized by his treatment. Our egos, which often swell to godlike size, are kept in check.

And sometimes, in the midst of such self-inflicted humility, we can hear something other than our own thoughts and selfish desires. A rumor of a real God. Faint, but audible.

For on the upside, the Marquis de God is a testimonial to divine power, of sorts. We have created a god we can revere because we have made ourselves powerless to do otherwise.

But this is not a true God at all. He is all too human. He behaves as if he had our ego. He loses his temper as we would.

This is a childish projection of fear. Fear not of God, but of our own inner savageness. We externalize it. Place it outside, so we don't have to admit to it inside.

But our making evil an act of retribution by a wrathful god does not explain evil. All we do is take it out of context. We create a duality out of a singular fabric that weaves light and dark, good and evil.

Carried to its extreme, evil, a mere thread in this fabric, is raised to the level of a force. Satans and antichrists incarnate in our consciousness. And it makes no difference whether you are a demon worshipper or a God fearer. The result of this kind of thinking is identical: Everything gets darker and darker, blacker and blacker, until light can re-enter only after the purification of apocalypse.

The cleansing love of mass destruction, as some believe. True sadomasochism!

Can we not stop turning paranoid delusions into spiritual revelations? Can we not stop invoking God's vindictiveness for everything that goes wrong in the world? And start blaming the consequences of our own moral decisions?

The alternative is a faith that worships punishment. And as a stupid way of thinking, the Marquis de God is a solid 10 on the Richter scale.

Stupid Way 4
God the Godfather

"So you want a favor. You say 'God, give me justice. Avenge my honor.' But this I cannot do.

"I've known you for many years. But when was the last time you paid me a visit?

"You do not treat me with respect."

Slump your shoulders. Bow your head. It's time to walk humbly before your Godfather. Il Capo della Famiglia. The Cosmic Consiglieri, Don Godleone.

He'll bless you on your wedding day. Help you break into show biz. Fulfill all your worldly desires. Even knock off your enemies. Provided, of course, you're willing to pay the price.

But if you're not willing, no matter. Don Godleone is prepared to make you an offer you can't refuse.

He carries you, and all his godchildren, in his vest pocket. Like so many nickels and dimes.

He doles out favors with one hand and carries a submachine gun in the other. To that extent, he is more balanced than other gods you may be familiar with. He has a light side and a dark side.

But Don Godleone is hardly a good model for the Universal God. He is interested only in *his* Family. Not the family of mankind.

Don Godleone is a primitive tribal god. A jealous, xenophobic deity so obsessed with his own domain that he will rub out anyone who dishonors him.

Nevertheless, he does have a redeeming personality. With this god, we can at least have some form of relationship. He is demanding, but approachable. We can talk to him, and he will counsel us. He is a godlike businessman with whom we can negotiate and strike a bargain.

But this is a limited relationship at best. Because pain, dismemberment, open threats of all kinds are implicit in his negotiating process. This is not a bargain, a *covenant*, in the biblical sense. Nor is the Don at all a God of Justice. God the Godfather is notorious. He demands respect from his people. He talks about codes of honor, but we cannot trust his word. We never know when he will turn on us. And bury us.

We ask him for favors. And we live in fear of the favor he will one day ask in return.

His end justifies his means. Because Don Godleone is nothing but a mobster. His apostles are his henchmen. And his only real concern is extending his influence and control.

This is a god who makes contracts but is outside his own laws.

Such a god is worse than immoral. He is amoral. And he can be appeased only by fanatical displays of ritual loyalty.

You must kiss his hand. You must kneel. You must huddle in the light of a full moon and make burnt offerings at his altar. You must even be prepared to sacrifice your first-born.

This is not a faith. It is extortion. A holy protection racket that mankind buys into.

Atheism toward this kind of god must never be regarded as apostasy. It is actually a sign of spiritual health. A sign that even with all our sacrifices, all our propitiation, we have not sacrificed our spirit.

Is there no god whose contract on our lives is a true covenant, worthy of respect? A god whose sense of give-and-take is bound by moral ethic? A god that does not need to be continually placated? A god with whom we can have a real, long-lasting relationship?

For although Don Godleone represents a certain advance in thought — the concept of a sharing, a mutuality, an agreement between God and man — it is nevertheless a stupid way of thinking. Because it is morally meaningless.

It is time we left the Family of the Don and found a better way to think about God and His requirements. One that isn't a cement straitjacket, a one-way ticket to the bottom of the river.

Stupid Way 5
God the General

"**S**tand at attention, you sonsabitches. I am your God. Lord and Commander. Now listen up!

"I will not give one hoot in hell for losers. You got that?

"So in my name, you will kick the enemy in the ass. You will go through him like crap through a goose.

"You will grease the treads of your tanks with his living guts. And I will be glorified."

Greetings. You have been drafted into one of the stupidest ways of thinking yet.

Say good-bye to the kids. Kiss the little woman for the last time. It's off to battle. He's got might. He's got right.

He is General God.

He's a nationalistic god, whose holy mission is to serve his country. Protect its honor. And defend its citizens.

But don't be swept away. This is not merely a god of defense, though he is often justified that way. General God is a self-righteous and meddlesome god. He is not content with holding his position. He wants to advance, and advance, and roll into any nation, at any time. To shove his views down your throat. To purify the earth of all infidels.

This is General Madness. A territorial maniac. A mercenary who can be employed by any nation for any cause.

He has blessed invasions of Ethiopia and Lebanon. He has consecrated the slaughter of Armenians and Vietnamese.

He is the commander of crusades. The leader of jihads. He guides kamikaze pilots to their death. He "makes the world safe for democracy." And recently, he commandeered the Iraqi annexation of Kuwait. This is a four-star bastardization of an ancient god, who chooses one group of people over another.

But he does not interact in history to establish moral law. Instead, he infects history with violence.

Yes, General God becomes a symbol of unity. To exalt some people and drive others apart.

He is exploited by governments to mobilize consciousness en masse. To turn ideology into theology.

This god grants us strength. To exalt our ego. To treat our enemies as subhuman. He teaches us to love our inhumanity.

This is hardly a god. This is a man-made expedient — an idolatrous creation whose job is simply to help us win, militaristically or economically. He is a warrior exhorting us to conquer for our country, in wars or in markets.

How wonderful it would be if we could indeed contain our moral dilemmas by force. How easy it would be to give up choice and just salute. How whole we all could feel if our divided loyalties could fuse into one divinely inspired movement. People, nation, and god advancing together as one front. Behind our flag. Behind a swastika.

But in the end, this god only leaves us dismayed by our destructiveness. Debased by our primitive behavior. And all too often, we find ourselves godless.

General God is a god who hates to lose. A god who, upon defeat, hides in a bunker until national pride surges again.

Can we not dispose of this idea of God in the latrine once and for all? Can we not stop worshiping in the church of the Purple Heart?

Is there no God who cannot be exploited to justify violent purposes? A God who can command morality? Not our military. A God that does not substitute a cheap, imperialistic nationalism for our true spirituality.

We will never find one unless we go AWOL from General God. We will stay stupid until we take the first step. And become conscientious objectors.

"City of Heaven, Department of Sanitation, God speaking. How may I help you?

"Two mortal sins for immediate pickup? One can of cardinal sins, one carton of venial? And an assortment of lust, greed, and sloth bundled and ready to go?

"Of course I can handle it! Just leave them on the side of the house. I'll be there Tuesday to take them away."

We've all got them. Stored up in the basement of our souls. Cluttering up our spirits. All that junk. All that gunk. Filthy, dirty, nasty, mean little sins.

But we don't have to carry them around, thank God. Not when we have a dumpster for a deity. God the Garbageman at your service. Or if you wish to sound more reverent, God the Sanitation Engineer.

You have a sin? God will cart it off to the great incinerator in the sky! Get out your trash bags!

You've sinned again? Oops! Well, have no fear. God will come back, and come back, and keep coming back, to make sure your spirit stays neat and tidy. All you have to do is 'fess up. And keep 'fessing up. Because this god is a bottomless pit. There's no limit to the refuse he can hold.

God the Garbageman is neither a dedicated civil servant nor a god. His job is simply to help mankind in what often seems like its most avid pursuit: escaping responsibility.

We've taken the marvelous concept of a forgiving God and distorted it completely. This is not the God who is beyond pagan acts of retribution. This is not the God who respects us so much He made us morally responsible. This is certainly not the God who guarantees us freedom of conscience even if we err.

God the Garbageman is simply a vehicle for an endless obsessive-compulsive ritual that would make Lady Macbeth seem pure. A kind of bulimia of the soul. Sin binging. And sin vomiting.

We connive and cheat people in business. And expect God to make us whole.

We have wild, erotic affairs and lie to our spouses. But we know God will make us clean.

Whom are we kidding? Only ourselves. Because we have no intention of stopping.

God allows us to have our cake and eat it too. We can be immoral, with confidence, knowing God will cleanse us. We can mistreat others, with impunity, knowing God will treat us kindly. We can indulge our greed, our sadism, our lusts, all the excesses of our all-too-human nature. Knowing God will indulge us in return.

Indeed, If God the Godfather is a Mafioso, then God the Garbageman is the Mafioso's god. Because for all practical purposes, he gives us permission to sin. And keep sinning.

He offers "fast-food" forgiveness. Just drive up any time, for his prepackaged blessing. What could be easier? With a god like this, who wouldn't risk enjoying a little sin?

Whatever momentary pangs of guilt or remorse we experience can be smoothly and comfortably eliminated. Yes, God has actually been reduced to a laxative. A simple home remedy for purging the human condition.

Is there no God whose forgiveness we can treat less frivolously? A God we don't just call up when we need to feel clean? A God who's more than a temporary break in an otherwise morally despicable life?

Is there no God who can inspire genuine reflection? Real, meaningful introspection? A God who can lay bare the pains of our souls and help heal them, by encouraging our own honesty?

Shouldn't a real God be worthy of *actions* of atonement, and not just words? Or, at least, an intent to not commit the same sin again?

But God the Garbageman only makes things worse for everyone. By making forgiveness so convenient, he allows us to take our own behavior for granted. We become so morally lazy we cease to grow as spiritual beings.

And we'll never grow . . . until we stop depending on someone else to dispose of our garbage for us . . . until we chuck God the Garbageman in the can and forget him.

Stupid Way 7
God the Macho Man

"You can best believe that He's a macho man. Hey . . . Hey . . . Hey . . . Hey . . . Hey Yahweh! Macho, Macho Man. I've got to be a Macho Man!"

Watch out, Burt Reynolds. Move over, Arnold Schwarzenegger. There's a new hunk in town.

He's a lean machine. Hard-nosed. Muscle-bound. Pumped with steroids and ready for action.

Wimps and women, be warned! It's God the Macho Man.

Boy, is this one of the stupidest ways to think about God ever! And one of the most common. He's spread throughout Judeo-Christian thinking like an epidemic.

All you have to do is look at the popular picture of God and you'll see the Macho Man's mystique. Not unlike Clark Gable, God is strong, silent, distant, demanding, obstinate, prone to anger. And, of course, controlling.

God the Macho Man controls religious dogma, rituals, and practice. He controls prayer books and biblical myths. He controls the priesthood, the ministry, and the rabbinate. Not to mention the conscience of people of both sexes.

God is Our King. Not our Queen, He is Our Father. Not Our Mother.

Yet, despite his pervasiveness, despite the overwhelming institutionalization and entrenchment of this idea, God the Macho Man is a fraud. A dangerous fraud.

He has been used to perpetrate the myth of male superiority for millennia. He has bolstered the influence and spheres of power of some of the most brutal males in history.

He has contaminated theology with sexist ideology, reflecting societal bias, not mature thought. For God the Macho Man is fictitious, an invention based on (excuse the pun, though it pleads our case even better) "manmade" standards.

Therefore, he is also one of the most idolatrous creations there is — a golden calf in man's clothing. Because God the Macho Man is clearly made in our image. Mankind's image. Or at least half of it.

And that can cause a lot of problems for the other half.

Little girls can grow up without being able to recognize themselves in God's image. They can have difficulty relating to God, the Man. Women who have "raised their consciousness" quickly become alienated from a male chauvinist in heaven. Even after a lifetime of devotion, they can suddenly find themselves in a faith crisis, unable to trust the god of a male cult.

On a practical level, women can be barred from deeper participation in their religion. They may be blocked from becoming priests or rabbis. And although there have been encouraging changes in recent years, there is still much dogma-based discrimination.

But it is not just women who are oppressed by a god like this. Everyone is. Because God the Macho Man may be big and impressive and strong, but he is not a true God. He's a half-truth, at most.

God the Macho Man is a freak of nature, an imbalance of cosmic proportions. He is incapable of demonstrating some of God's most marvelous qualities, many of the qualities that distinguish Him from more primitive pagan gods.

A Macho God does not nurture. A Macho God does not heal. A Macho God is not caring, or tender. He bestows his love more in the form of discipline than concern.

In fact, considering that these are some of the most important attributes of God, it might be more accurate to refer to Him as Goddess.

And let's face it, even for men, God the Macho Man is hardly a good role model. He is not a real man at all, but an unrealistic, polarized caricature of maleness, devoid of all sensitivities. As oppressive to men as to women.

There is real danger in allowing society's standards to determine the personality of God. Standards that can be undermined and manipulated by any power elite to subordinate whole segments of a population.

Where is the God who created "Adam" — Hebrew for "mankind?" The God of men *and* women. Where is our real God hiding?

We'll never find Him until we take God the Macho Man and (gulp!) neuter him.

Stupid Way 8
God the Political Candidate

He's shaking hands. He wants your vote. Wants you in his hip pocket. And he'll do anything to get you there. Including lie, cheat, and swindle.

Yes, now God's running for the highest office. But if you know what's good for you, you'll run the other way.

God the Political Candidate's platform is simple. He wants to instill moral purity into each and every individual, whether he or she wants it or not. He's on the domestic warpath to see that every soul follows the correct path. The only question is, "Whose path"? For him the answer is cut and dried: *His*.

Yes, this is the God of the majority, or the imagined majority, moral, or otherwise. The God who is out to convert — or eradicate — sinners who lead our country astray.

His tactics are anything but morally pure, let alone consonant with our national values. For God the Political Candidate is simply a demagogue. Of the worst kind.

He does not persuade, but condemns. He does not respect your freedom to disagree. Or your right to believe differently.

He displays a total disregard for freedom of conscience. A total disrespect for individual choice. And a complete abhorrence for religious beliefs that differ from his.

In the guise of a true believer, in the guise of a loyal citizen, he is simply coercing people to believe what he wants them to believe. He is a one-issue candidate. One view. One belief. And anyone who doesn't agree with him will not be tolerated. Individual differences are to be feared. Because they express doubt, sacrilegious doubt, in god's political agenda. And for that we deserve more than to lose an election.

Indeed, God the Political Candidate is a vicious political animal who will stop at nothing to enforce his political theology. But, before we condemn him so quickly, and therefore do the same thing to him that he does to us, we'd better think a little more deeply.

If God exists, shouldn't He be the basis of the moral principles we integrate into our legal structures? Shouldn't our legislators allow God to guide their hands? Shouldn't God be the rock upon which the foundation of our society is built? Shouldn't there be one divinely inspired policy implemented across the board?

If so, isn't anyone who disagrees with this policy a traitor to both God and country? Isn't anyone who expresses a different belief, a different opinion, or has a different faith undermining the establishment of God's Perfect Political System, commonly called His Kingdom? Indeed, what's so bad about God the Political Candidate? He seems the model God, for the model citizen, embodying the model faith.

The problem is the very nature of *faith*. What makes it faith. Faith, to be faith, must be more than the blind adherence to any one belief. It must be more than the dogmatic acceptance of a party line. To be truly faithful, an individual must *choose* to believe. Faith can come only after deep introspection and self-reflection. It is a delicate, precious gift that must be cherished and respected because it comes from deep within the individual's soul.

Therefore, *there can be no faith without freedom.* Which is why God the Political Candidate is actually undermining faith rather than upholding it. He has violated freedom of conscience, the very basis of the faith experience.

This is abuse of power — plain and simple. And God the Political Candidate leads people like sheep to the slaughter. No one stops to question his authority. No one asks his qualifications. God the Political Candidate rallies people with a high-minded, know-it-all attitude that presumes complete personal knowledge of God's Will. In essence, God the Political Candidate is a cult leader. He has substituted his version of earthly authority for God's authority. He has made his word equivalent to God's Holy Word. In a nutshell, he has taken the name of the real God in vain.

He is a false idol. A true traitor to God and country, opening the door to the destruction of democracy and the institution of divinely-inspired dictatorships. It is exactly this that the idea of separation of church and state was intended to prevent.

Can any leader ever take the place of God? Should we ever trust any individual so much that we sacrifice freedom of choice and individual conscience in the act of worship?

What is the borderline between divine authority and mortal authority? How can we fuse them in principle, without confusing them in practice? These are the issues that God the Political Candidate really speaks to.

But we won't face them honestly until we stop casting our ballots for this political sham of a deity.

Stupid Way 9
God as Mom Nature

Well, we can stop searching for God. He's been there all the time.

God's been blossoming in the fields. Grazing in the pastures. He's been hiding under a rock. Stuck inside a glacial fissure.

God's been speaking to us through the mouths of volcanoes. His words have been babbling to us in brooks.

God is the birds and the bees. The flies and mosquitoes. He's the mold growing on bread. The lint accumulating in our navels.

Yes, we've found our god. The god of hippies and flower-power. The pantheistic god of everything natural. Dear, sweet, charming Mom Nature.

Makes sense, doesn't it? After all, Mom Nature is mysterious. She works miracles. She is powerful, yet balanced. Subtle in her ways, yet majestic.

She has a definite wisdom to her nature. And, as with God, it's not nice to fool her. It can have dire consequences.

But despite these convincing similarities, if you believe Mom Nature is God Himself, it's really you who are getting fooled. Because *she* is a god who's everywhere but nowhere.

As perfect as she seems, Mom Nature leaves a lot of questions open. And the answers, my friend, aren't blowing in the wind.

For one thing, where did Nature come from? Who created her?

Nature couldn't be God. She put on her bonnet only *after* the big bang. She was born out of nothing, along with everything else in creation. Though God may be seen to work through nature, He could never be considered merely nature itself.

For another thing, if Mom Nature is God, then how come we have the power to destroy her? You'd think any God of ours would be more powerful than we are.

And then, there's the ever-troubling question of evil.

As God, Mom Nature could explain *natural* evils like the AIDS virus, Mt. Vesuvius, the bubonic plague, and the San Francisco earthquakes. But she is mute when it comes to explaining where *moral* evil comes from.

Murder, child abuse, war, inhumanities and sins of all kinds, are simply not part of a natural ecosystem. They are outside her domain. So naturally, she could never be considered a true God. Of human beings, that is.

On the contrary, God as Mom Nature could only be the god of everything in nature, except us. Our egos, our goals, our drives for perfection, our acquisitiveness, our inquisitiveness, our creativity, our intellectual gifts, our capacity for self-sacrificial love, our *spirituality*, are all things this simple god of nature cannot account for.

Any God of ours must be conscious of our moral dilemma. He must be able to explain why we continue to strive, but suffer. He must be able to account for the nature of our lives — why we feel so alienated, so ostracized from the Garden of Eden. And ideally, He should be able to offer us some ray of hope.

But to say that the idealized goodness and unity of nature are identical to the Unity of the One God is baloney. And dangerously close to idolatry. It is merely one step away from collapsing into multiple gods of wind, rain, and sun.

God may have created Mom Nature to be His right-hand gal. And for that she deserves a lot more deference than we are currently showing her on the planet.

But as a god in her own right, as our real God, she just wilts.

Stupid Way 10
God the Master of Ceremonies

on't touch that dial! It's time for the God Show. Starring your Eternal favorite. The inimitable Ruler Himself. The Lord of entertainment. The King of opening monologues. Your Master of Ceremonies. . .

Heeeeeeeerrrrrrrrrre's God!!

[APPLAUSE]

[LOUDER]

Of all our stupid ways of thinking about God, this is by far the stupidest. So stupid it deserves to be last. Because absolutely no thought whatsoever goes into this notion.

You've got a wedding? a bar mitzvah? a confirmation? a christening? a circumcision? God the Master of Ceremonies is the ultimate party dude.

It makes no difference the last time you stepped into a church or synagogue. It doesn't matter when you last prayed. Or even whether you believe. Because God the M.C. can be hired by anyone, for any occasion. He's Rent-a-God!

God the Master of Ceremonies is invoked with all the pomp and circumstance, all the apparent reverence, rites, and incantations befitting the worship of a true God. He may appear holy. But he is hollow.

Because God the M.C. is just a sham. His ceremonies are shows. And often, the more money you donate to your church or synagogue, the better the seats.

God is being exploited to provide an illusion, the security of tradition. To bolster intergenerational family ties, to force bonding between infants and society, between men and women.

He helps people maintain nominal religious affiliation, with no relation to spirituality. And without real faith, strong personal commitment, and sincere religious motivation, God is reduced to a viewer spectacle, a façade.

God the M.C. comes out, does his act, then retires off-stage.

The meaning and relevance of the idea of One God is lost. Devotion is dead. What is important is that the correct words are spoken, the right rituals are performed, the necessary prayers offered, the traditional vows taken.

God has been rendered a spiritless ceremonialist. A show-biz god. All that remains is a shell of faith that in the absence of sentimentality would crumble to dust.

Indeed, God the Master of Ceremonies is even more empty of spirituality than atheism is. Atheism can be equally blind, but it never pretends to be something else. At least it's honest.

For many, the sheer hypocrisy of this begins very early. A child is born, and his parents suddenly feel the urge to drop their tennis rackets and get in some old-time religion.

This may be done unconsciously, out of deep guilt, with considerable social and family pressure. Or perhaps parents are sincerely trying to give their children something of value, permanence, meaning. An identity.

As noble as their desires sound, frequently parents are not so emphatic about the importance of God in their own lives. And their religion is seldom practiced at home.

Just imagine how it looks to a young child when his mother and father themselves do not take seriously the faith they are force-feeding. It is enough to make any god unworthy of belief.

What more classic example than the modern-day bar mitzvah boy, who starts Hebrew school at eight, memorizes his lines, and bows out of religious life at thirteen. Along with his family's temple membership!

This kind of thing has become a tradition in many religions. Because God the M.C. is symptomatic of how passively faith is practiced. Especially in liberal religions that don't keep the fires of hell stoked.

Congregations have become more like audiences that need to be entertained. They want God in a form that's comfortable. Easy to swallow. With words about sin and spiritual responsibility kept to a tolerable minimum.

Churches and synagogues have atrophied into singles clubs and bingo parlors. They have been emptied of spirit. And God the M.C. shows up simply to administer the occasional formalities and rituals required. He sanctifies without substance.

Granted, God the M.C. does demonstrate a talent for bringing people together. Granted, he can help people feel close. Many times a "spirit" can be felt when people gather for a special occasion in love. And these opportunities are far too precious in life to quibble over inconsistencies.

Nonetheless, making God a game show host for the three or four formal rites of passage preserved in middle-class life is no game at all. It's a desecration.

This show of religiosity may be a real crowd pleaser. But God the Master of Ceremonies is a buffoon.

Where Did We Go Astray?

Where Did We Go Astray?

So we've smashed some icons, slaughtered some sacred cows, and taken some pot shots at Providence. But you must admit, when it comes to thinking about God, we're all a little stupid — authors included.

Even if we missed some stupid ways of thinking about God, look around. The world is full of them. And new ones crop up every day.

But it's not our purpose to document them. Nor would we ever, even in our playfulness, want to make anyone, let alone ourselves, feel dumb.

A stupid way of thinking about God is not necessarily dumb at all. It's not necessarily false either. It's simply incomplete. It explains some things, but not others. It solves some problems, but not other problems. And often, it creates a mess of problems of its own.

51

However, the road to the smart ways of thinking about God is not always smooth. And before we start out, maybe we should get better acquainted with some of the potholes along the way. Some of the fundamental theological head-bangers that make smart thinking about God so difficult.

❖   ❖   ❖

See Dick. See Jane. See Spot. As children, we learned to describe the world around us as we saw it — the objects, the people, the places. To a child's mind, seeing is believing. If we saw it, it *was*.

But it didn't take long before we learned that seeing wasn't all there was to believing. We learned we can't always trust our eyes, or our ears, or our touch. Our view of reality is limited by the range of our senses.

Needless to say, for an invisible God, proof can't be as simple as "See God." In fact, it's actually quite the reverse. Because when it comes to God, believing is seeing. This may sound like a cosmic Catch-22, but when you think about it, it makes sense. We never discovered the atom until we began to believe it could exist. We never discovered bacteria until we began to believe illness could have a scientific explanation. For discovering, uncovering, and exploring the hidden, more subtle realities beneath the surface of things, believing is seeing. Or at least the beginning of seeing.

And it's really no different for discovering God.

But let's face it, it isn't easy to think about God when you're human. Like it or not, we're severely limited by our genus and species. We can think about God, or anything, only in human terms. We can create only human ideas about God. We can relate to Him only through human concepts, human theories, human pictures. We can describe God only by human language and through human experience.

So of course, there's plenty of room for contamination. There's a lot of opportunity to superimpose our view of ourselves on top of God, a lot of opportunity to accidently fashion God after ourselves.

Alas, we're stuck. There's no way we can ever think about God that will not make Him appear human to some extent. Even if we conceive of Him as some great disembodied force, we can still only conceive of a "force" as we understand it in human terms — as lightning, electromagnetism, gravitational fields, and so on. But we need not apologize for that. After all, we are what we are. Still, we are bound to make a few human mistakes.

To err is definitely human. But somewhere you've got to draw the line. There are *some* ways to think about God, as human as they are, that are simply false. That's why the Bible, especially the Old Testament, talked so much about idols, or graven images. That's why, back in ancient times, making *any* image of God was strictly taboo.

God forbid we, in our bumbling human way, should create a picture so beautiful we pray to it *as* God, instead of a representation of God.

God forbid we should create an image, an idea, a theory, so captivating we mistake it for God Himself. That's the idolator's error. We worship our creation instead of God. We worship *our* idea instead of God. In essence, what this really means is we're worshipping ourselves!

If we have a false sense of self, we cannot help but create a false god. If we have a false sense of values, we cannot help but create a god that's worthless. But rather than realize the problem lies in us, we pin it on God. Excuses,

excuses! It's our dishonesty toward ourselves that creates our disillusionment with God.

If we're serious about thinking about God, we also have to think more seriously about ourselves. If we really want to delve into the mystery of God, and get reliable answers, we've got to look inward, find the real McCoy, the genuine article, our true selves. We've got to have the courage to grow psychologically. To improve ourselves. To heal ourselves. To expose all our inner falsehoods to the light of day.

We have to do a lot of personal work. And the more we clean up our act, the cleaner our view of God.

But admittedly, if our view of God changes as we do, we're left with some very uncomfortable questions: What is truth? Whose truth is truth? Can we ever know for sure that truth even exists?

These days we tend to look to science for the answers. It searches for truth about how nature operates. Its theories and laws explain a host of phenomena. But science tends to ignore the other side of truth. Philosophical truth. Ethical truth. Moral truth. Emotional truth. The theories and laws that explain nature's most baffling phenomenon: people.

How should one person treat another? What is the correct way to offer charity? Or deal with guilt? How do we live for ourselves without becoming selfish? How do we live for others without becoming martyrs?

Can science answer these questions? Can any experiment, no matter how exacting, measure the human heart? If it could, would the world be in such a pickle? Who could look at the threat of atomic warfare, ecological destruction, urban decay, and not question the truth of science? Isn't it time we admit that science, too, has earned its share of doubts?

On the other hand, is religion any better? Didn't it perpetuate a lot of bigotry and superstition in the name of truth? Didn't it often encourage poverty and ignorance as a sign of devoutness? Didn't it frequently require us to trade real-world happiness for other-world rewards?

This is why the idea of God, the pure and uncontaminated *idea* of God, is such a radical notion. Despite competing claims of truth by religion and science, the idea of God asserts that there must be, can be, only one truth: God. And this Truth is the source of both scientific truths *and* human truths. God is the source of the laws of nature *and* the laws of the human spirit.

The idea of God means there can be only *one complete truth. One ultimate truth.* Science, religion, all individual truths, are at best only partly true. Parts of the elephant. Not the whole. God and Truth are inseparable. They are one and the same. What is Truth? In truth, only God could possibly know.

No matter what we believe about God, or don't believe about God, there will always be huge gaps in our knowledge. No belief, no faith, no theory, no ideology, no religion could ever be so complete, so true that it could be considered God Himself. God is just too big to be contained by man's thoughts. No one can know God simply by contemplating, pondering, or reflecting. All thoughts about God are just ways of conceptualizing Him, attempts — meager attempts — to conceive of something that is by nature inconceivable.

God could never be carved up like a turkey to serve our own intellectual needs and still remain God. So to some extent, all ways of thinking about God are stupid.

Then what are the smart ways to think about God? Are there any at all?

Smart Ways to Think About GOD

What's Smart?

here is no priest, no rabbi, no minister, no saint, no New Age master or old-age prophet who can answer this question completely. We are all like good little scouts practicing theological knots, hoping to win ourselves a merit badge from the Almighty.

Thinking about God isn't easy at all when God is beyond thought. In fact, it's almost impossible. There's *no* way of thinking that can make God understandable. But if that's what we mean by a smart way to think about God, forget it. Pack it in! The journey's over. The only perfect answer is God Himself.

So why bother searching at all? Because if God exists, if there is some ultimate answer, some ultimate reality, beyond the one our senses acknowledge, then the consequences for our lives are enormous indeed. Our purpose in life can then no longer be justified by *my* wants, *my* feelings, *my* needs, or *my* desires, but only by *His* wants, *His* feelings, *His* needs, and *His* desires. Or ideally, both our wants together.

Why bother? The reason is dumb simple: If God exists and we don't live as if He exists, then we are living a lie.

We may attempt to escape into practical matters, but in the emptiness of a painful moment, after the despair of a failure, or on a quiet, starlit night when we are most vulnerable to ourselves, we have no answer for a question even more basic than "Why bother?" We have no answer for "Why?" That is the importance of God. And that's as important for the atheist as for the believer. As crucial to the scientist as to the theologian.

However, if God is to have any meaning at all, He cannot just be pondered. He must be lived. God must be *experienced*. That's what we mean by a smart way to think about God.

A smart way is an idea that you can experience. Not just with your mind but with your life. It's an idea you don't have to shed like a snakeskin. It's an idea you can grow with. And one that grows with you. It's an idea you can commit a lifetime to, without running into like a brick wall.

Smart ways of thinking about God expand and change. They also expand and change us. They deepen with life experience. And deepen the experience of life. They begin to acquaint us with a core of unshakable Truth by opening our hearts to a reality that mere thought alone cannot understand. However, they must never leave our intelligence standing outside, begging to get in. They must be big enough to include every part of us, even our sense of reason.

Smart ways of thinking about God should allow us to catch a glimpse of God's reflection as He passes by. And in that reflection we should also catch a glimpse of ourselves. Not our false selves, but our true selves, our complete selves.

Smart ways of thinking about God should allow us to experience not only God but also the meaning and purpose of our lives, the lives of others, and everything that makes up the miracle of existence.

What's smart? Simply, a way to think about God that makes us feel whole. A way that is so all-embracing, all-powerful, it makes us feel complete.

Nevertheless, after so many stupid ways of thinking, smart ways can seem a bit elusive. So maybe it's best just to start out fresh. Maybe we should go back to a smarter kind of Sunday school. Maybe we should approach God, once again, like a child. With a clean slate. With a clear, impressionable yet rational mind. And with an open, innocent, willing heart.

Smart Way 1
God Is the Beginning

A smart way to think about God begins with God Himself. Because God *is* the beginning. The beginning of the beginning. The absolute beginning. It's well worth repeating.

A deceptively simple notion. But a monumental concept, if you come to grips with it. Though it's not easy.

It means that before anything existed, there was still something. And that something is commonly called God.

Before the big bang, before the space-time continuum, before energy and matter, before our universe, or any universe. Even before George Burns. God was there.

It means that this universe didn't just happen out of nothing. It's no chance occurrence. No coincidence. No celestial hiccup. It happened out of God.

God is the Origin of all existence. He pointed the universe in one direction. Shot what physicists call "the arrow of time." Established a flow. From beginning. To end.

Somehow, He is responsible for all that exists, has ever existed, will ever exist, or could ever exist. Somehow the universe — past, present, and future — is inextricably joined to God's Being.

It is a Being that is Pure. A reality so basic, so fundamental, it cannot be split into simpler components. It cannot be placed in an accelerator and reduced to a particle zoo.

God is an indivisible Whole. A Whole that is beyond all the opposites of our reality. A Whole that is beyond protons and electrons. Beyond positives and negatives. Beyond mortal loves and hates.

And yet, somehow, all of those things are part of Him. Every force in the universe . . . He embraces them all. Tucks them in under His coat, because they were born out of the fabric of His Being. Being that is Timeless. Or, if you wish to sound more traditional, Eternal. Without beginning. Without end. Unbounded. Unlimited. Except by Himself.

His is also a Being of Infinite Potential. All possibilities — even those as yet unrealized — are part of His Nature. Everything conceivable and inconceivable.

Now this is a God! Once you've met Him, there can't be anyone else. The universe is just not big enough. Here is a God that cannot be made out of "stuff." His atoms were never part of galactic nebulae, or the dust of comets. He never simmered in the cosmic crockpot that gave birth to the universe. He was the cook.

Here is a God that cannot be shaped by the hands of time. Or the hands of man. He can never be fashioned in our image. He can hardly be imagined; He existed before imagination.

Here is a God who could never be the wind, the sun, the stars. They're just fragments of His reality. Insignificant bits of His Total Reality, blinked into existence, in the beginning.

This is the only God that could ever be a real God. Because He is Super-God. Bigger and better than them all. The only kind of God able to leap over all idols.

This is the only kind of God that can never be proven false. Oh, you can debate Him, ad infinitum. But you can't prove Him false. He is beyond human concept altogether.

Yep, He's one of a kind. A true Original.

But it took thousands of years for man to pay Him His due. It was millennia before mankind could put aside the mumbo jumbo and recognize, or conceive of, a God this sublime.

Well, birds gotta fly, and man had to grow. Our consciousness had to evolve. Our awareness had to become more refined. We had to leave the primitive thoughts of the pagan behind.

Nevertheless, it was worth the journey to get to this beginning. The beginning of one of the smartest ways to think about God ever: One, sole, singular, complete, independent, unique, exceptional Deity. The Source of all.

It's a revolutionary concept introduced by Judaism, popularized by Christianity and Islam. It's called *monotheism*.

It's an idea that changed the world. And everyone in it.

Smart Way 2
God Is Living

If this entity, this God, were *just* the Origin, *just* the Infinite Sum of everything, it would not be God at all. It could be another universe, from which everything was born. It could be a black hole. Or the grand unified field, which modern physics searches for like the Holy Grail. But it would not be God.

These are just ideas, descriptions — albeit complicated mathematical descriptions — of primordial reality. They may help us grapple with our limitations; they may help us conceptualize the "infinite." But they are still only human concepts, objects created by our own minds.

If we think of these descriptions as supreme knowledge, which these days people are apt to do, we have in essence reverted to a different kind of idol worship. We have constructed a calf from numbers instead of gold.

Because if God is God, if He existed before time and space, He cannot be anyone's object at all. He's got to be subject. And to be a subject, God must be alive. Indeed, either God is living, or the whole idea of God is dead. Or pure illusion.

But what do we mean by *living*? Certainly God doesn't breathe in air, digest His food, or reproduce. Nor does He grow seasonally and need to be transplanted.

By saying God is living, we mean that this God, this Infinity that permeates everything, possesses a quality that distinguishes subjects from objects, animate from inaminate.

A strange, wonderful quality called *consciousness*.

God, to be God, must be conscious. But He must possess far more than vegetative consciousness; God, to be God, must be at least as conscious as we. He must not be merely conscious, but self-conscious. Conscious of Himself. God must be aware of who He is. His thoughts. His feelings. His desires. (Not that His process of thinking, feeling, or desiring could ever be said to be the same as ours.)

God must somehow be able to mirror His own mind. He, too, must have a self-concept. But unlike ours, His must be purer, cleaner, infinite, or He could not be our God.

God must have a self-concept that is not based on self-deceit, one that doesn't reflect in a carnival mirror, distorted by repressed pains or swollen ego. And of course, His consciousness must be considerably more conscious than ours.

We may have trouble staying aware of our next-door neighbor. But God's awareness must be all-embracing. It must fathom the depths of His own infinities. It must also extend to all creation, enveloping and permeating everything living and nonliving — throughout all time, and beyond all time.

Indeed, this Consciousness *is* His Being, His Nature. It is the "substance" from which everything else is made. Organic or inorganic, it was formed from, formed by, formed out of His Consciousness.

This Living Awareness, the *Living* Origin of everything — that is what is meant by God.

Who is He? Who knows?

Because it is impossible to describe Him fully by human concepts, we must often resort to analogies. God is like this. God is like that. He is a seed, a womb, a cradle, a father, a mother, a fountain, a root, an ocean. That's as far as even the most renowned theologians get.

There are fancier words like omnipresent, omniscient, ineffable. And other words, used so ritualistically, so carelessly, that we forget, or never really understand, their meanings.

Some people, like Buddhists, avoid complications completely, with non-descripts like "That" or "Such." But whether it's this, that, or the other thing, it is hardly emotionally satisfying.

Nevertheless, there is one word, used by everyone in the world. It's not scientifically accurate, nor it is mathematically precise. It's hardly as perfect as the God it is meant to convey. But at least it works. It has withstood the test of time. That word is *spirit*.

Nobody knows exactly what spirit is. But then, if no one really knows what God is, maybe *spirit* is pretty good, after all.

Spirit. God is Living Spirit.

We're getting smarter every day.

Smart Way 3
God Is the Creator

ne thing is certain: Any Spirit with this kind of awareness has got to have one heck of an I.Q. He's got to be the Ultimate Prodigy.

God must be supremely intelligent to be God. And if we look at His creation, we should be able to see this intelligence at work. We should be able to see it in the ingenious sequencing of amino acids that is DNA. We should be able to study it in the structure and dance of subatomic particles.

We should be able to witness God's intelligence on a cosmic scale. From quasars and pulsars to the "simple" rotation of our troubled little planet. Everything in the universe, and in all possible universes, should vibrate with this intelligence. All phenomena, even if not completely understandable, should appear to unfold in an orderly and methodic fashion.

Our ever-increasing understanding of nature and the mechanics of Creation should not encourage atheism. On the contrary, it should discourage it. It only confirms that there is some intelligence — superior intelligence — that has organized and designed reality as a singular, integrated whole.

This intelligence is not a religious myth. It exists. It is a fact. A mysterious, marvelous fact, more obvious in this century than ever before.

Indeed, the more we understand, the more it is clear that God knows what the hell He's doing. Because along with the universe were created precise laws to govern it, to explain the relationship and behavior of its parts. And these laws seem to apply to everything in existence, living or not.

Truly, the whole universe seems to be thoroughly thought out. Not with cold, calculating logic, or the tortured rumination of a dusty academician. But with unbelievable flair. For God is not just an Intelligent Spirit, but a Creative Spirit. Perhaps that's why He's so difficult to understand. All creative spirits, whether Mozart, Einstein, or Frank Zappa, can seem a little odd, if not enigmatic. Hard for mere mortals to relate to.

Nevertheless, without that immortal spark, without creativity, God could not have inspired anyone. And everywhere we look we are inspired. By beauty. Flawless beauty. From the color and tenderness of a flower to the magnificent swirling of red and orange on Jupiter.

But God's creativity cannot just end with a singular act of Creation. Because a Living God must always live to create. He cannot perform once and fade away like an old vaudeville star.

God, a Living God, must be eternally creative. New forms, new galaxies, new phenomena, must always arise. If this weren't so, the universe would stay the same. God would be stagnant, or dead.

But that doesn't happen. The cosmos changes constantly. A new drama unfolds every nanosecond. It is a process that cannot cease.

It is the process of *evolution*.

What is evolution, if not the most definitive proof of God's creativity? Creativity that began with the big bang. Creativity that transformed a planet with a primitive atmosphere of ammonia, methane, and water vapor. Creativity that took the sludge of an ancient sea and formed the most miraculous thing of all: life.

Yes, life was created out of matter. But matter, and the universe, were created from Living Spirit.

And over the eons, matter was arranged even more creatively, even more ingeniously, until the Spirit within it became more obvious. Until it possessed a consciousness that seemed independent of everything around it. Until it "breathed" Spirit, and made mere matter seem spiritless by comparison.

Life was indeed a product of evolution. But evolution is not a theory. It is more likely the hand of God. God the Creator.

Smart Way 4
God Is the Creator of Creators

S o God kept his hands busy, creative sort that He was. Until one day, a trifling million years ago (by geological standards), a new species appeared.

It didn't look all too different. It was a little less hairy. Seemed more comfortable standing on its hind legs. But it still had a backbone, a protruding jaw, a bulging forehead, and opposable thumbs. Like a chimpanzee or a gorilla.

Yet this ape was different. More special than King Kong. More talented than the Marquis Chimps.

In the future, it would go bowling. It would create "disco." it would climb up corporate ladders instead of trees.

Its brain was larger. The frontal lobes were more pronounced. And its consciousness was more advanced. It was not just conscious, but self-conscious. Aware of itself.

Indeed, this consciousness was so highly evolved it could be said to resemble God's. To be created in His image.

This creature, of course, is no other than *Homo sapiens*. Man.

Like God, man is intelligent. He can understand himself and the things around him. His intelligence allows him to extend dominion over the whole planet. And into the solar system. It allows him to influence life and even tinker with the genetic code.

Intelligence gives man the extraordinary ability to control, to a certain extent, his own evolution. To improve himself. To heal himself. Intelligence has even granted him a measure of immortality. He can educate himself. Teach his children. And his knowledge and experience can live on after him.

Like God, man is also creative. He invents. He builds. He makes objects in his own image.

Yep, man, like God, is a creator. And, like the Creator Himself, man possesses a quality that is truly godlike. The source of his dignity, and his suffering. *Man has free will.*

He is relatively free to make choices. He can determine what he wants to do, or not to do. He can say yea, or nay.

Man is not totally a slave to his animal instincts. He doesn't live just for food or shelter. He can strive for something far less concrete. A concept. An abstraction. Like democracy. Like communism. Or, for that matter, like God. Man can live for higher truths, nobler ideals. And even if they're unattainable, he will work relentlessly toward them. He will strive to "reach that unreachable star." Because he has an extraordinary virtue: faith. Or is it stubbornness?

But man is also free to ignore lofty ideals. He can devote his life to fattening himself or his wallet. He is free to create his own hell.

Yes, man is a colossus, poised with godlike capabilities but still feeling an all-too-human burden of choice. He can choose to create or to destroy. He can choose for good or for evil. One from column A. Two from column B.

Yet all too often, despite his extraordinary accomplishments, man feels the strain of this burden, the weight of his own potential, his own humanity. He may vault the heavens, but he still cruises bars on Saturday night. He can build machines that were once science fiction, but he can't get his emotions in gear.

Man can feel alienated from himself and often from others. He feels a separation between the ideals he can conceive and the reality he lives. In this distance from himself, man can feel even further separated from the ultimate ideal: the Wholeness and Goodness of God.

In theological circles this separation is called *sin*. A useful concept, but one that has been abused. It has perpetrated untold guilt and has contributed to tremendous emotional damage. And not without the help of some careless clergy.

Nevertheless, we all must admit to this feeling of separation, this inner sense of alienation. There's a gulf between our thoughts and our actions. Between God and us. And whatever you call it, this gulf exists. It is real. So it, too, must be part of creation.

Does God have something in mind? Either he has, or he's not only created a creator, but a lot of problems, too.

God Has a Plan

L adies and Gentlemen. Welcome to the wrestling match to end all wrestling matches. In this corner: good. In the opposite corner: evil.

Today, the Sons of Light will do battle with the Sons of Darkness. It's Gog vs. Magog. The Hulk vs. The Ultimate Warrior. A true spectacle, for a spectacular prize: the fate of the world.

It would indeed be wonderful if God could put on His wrestling tights and fight man's battles for him. What a great way to show His concern! But there's a hitch. God can't.

Sounds strange, doesn't it — an all-powerful God that can't do everything?

You see, God has a plan. But that plan includes Him, too. And even God must play by God's rules. He can't break them like Don Godleone.

One of those rules was that God made man special. He made him a creator, gave him free will, responsibility for his decisions and his actions.

God can't just decide to swoop down and make our lives perfect. That would be an insult against our humanity, our nature. It would violate the very free spirit He gave us.

God's plan must begin with respect for the creators He created. He must allow man his rope, even if he hangs himself. Or there can be no possibility of a relationship between them. God can't just give us choice and then take it away. He'd have broken His Word. He would have violated His own Spirit, too. And what kind of God would that be? Just someone you couldn't trust. And any plan God has is meaningless unless we can trust Him.

What is that plan? In a word, *perfection*.

If God comes close to having any fault at all, it's that He's a perfectionist. God wants perfection, but not our concept of perfection. He doesn't care if Islam reigns. Or Judaism. Or Christianity. Or Zoroastrianism. He's everyone's God. He wants perfection for everyone. He doesn't want material perfection, because if He did, He would have left matter as matter, and not organized it into anything quite as imperfect as life.

God wants spiritual perfection. He wants the world to be as perfect as the Spirit that conceived it. To be as perfect as He is perfect.

Said another way, God wants everything in the universe to return to the Origin. That doesn't mean He wants to destroy it, disassemble every atom and start afresh in some apocalyptic nightmare. It means He wants it to return to the Origin of the origin. To Spirit. To God. The ideal Perfection.

God wants us to become so acutely aware of our divine origin that we act it. He wants us to become divine creators in our own right. To live in accordance with the laws He created with Creation.

God can help somewhat. He can inspire revelations like the teachings of Moses, Jesus, Buddha, or Mohammed. But God cannot force us to be moral. He cannot make our choices for us. He cannot, and will not, interfere with our free will. Or freeze our hands to prevent us from creating evil. Or free our souls from the divisions within us.

God has no intention of creating a world filled with evil. He's not the Marquis de God. But clearly, by creating us, our God left room for evil — the evil he gave us freedom to create.

That's why God's plan requires our cooperation. It's not enough for us to blindly trust Him, like Little Mary Sunshine. God has to trust us, too.

This is the meaning of the biblical concept of *covenant.* Whether it's old or new, borrowed or blue, a covenant is truly a marriage between God and man. A moral contract to work hand in hand for the perfection of the world. An agreement that it is not just God's responsibility but also ours.

In a very real sense, there are two creators. God and mankind. We are cocreators in the world. And ironically, an all-powerful God must depend on us.

But even if everyone, everywhere — every race, creed, and nationality — cooperated with God, could we really achieve perfection?

Yes, but within limits.

Certainly, most of the evil in the world would be eliminated. Poverty and cruelty would disappear. Swords would be beaten into plowshares. But even if moral evil ended, there would still be natural evil. A volcano could erupt and decimate a village. An unexpected drought could cause a food shortage. There could still be car accidents, earthquakes, disease. Tragedy would still be there. Bad things could continue to happen to good people.

Why? Because the world is incomplete. We could not expect a world that is not finished to be perfectly stable. Any more than we could expect a table with three legs to stay balanced.

Even if we all did our jobs as cocreators, the rest would be up to God. Only He could eliminate natural evil. Only He could complete the process of evolution and make perfection a reality.

Ultimately how and when this happens remains a mystery. Not an ordinary mystery, like the ones that occupy our science and philosophies, but an impenetrable mystery. We cannot know. We have no choice but to accept it as an article of faith.

That is the mystery of *redemption*. That is what trust in God is all about.

Nevertheless, it could all happen a lot sooner, if we all chipped in and did our part. Because even natural evil can be lessened. We don't have to complicate famines by a lack of sharing; we don't have to add moral insult to natural injury.

There are those who believe in a fallen angel, cast out of God's Kingdom, banished from His perfection, causing mischief in the world. If that angel exists, he is certainly man.

When we start doing our job, then the world will be prepared to return to its original perfection. That's when God can live up to His end of the bargain. The universe, along with mankind, can be redeemed, and the envisioned Messianic age can come.

This will indeed require a battle. But it will be a wrestling match between us and our conscience. It must take place in the arena of each human heart.

Smart Way 6
God Is Personal

I t's time to stop flying around the universe, ferreting out God's intentions, and come back down to earth. We may be creators, too, but God doesn't have to earn a living. He doesn't have to pay off a car loan. Or go through the pain of a divorce.

Sooner or later we all have to put up or shut up. Stop thinking about God, and start acting. If you believe in God, you can't spend an eternity sitting on the fence. You have to commit. Either we start bringing God into our personal lives and start *living* Him, or even our smartest lessons will remain hopelessly stupid.

If you believe in God, He must become a practical matter. As important as the price of beans or oil. God must have real consequences for your life or you are, to put it bluntly, a hypocrite.

If you believe in God, you can't do anything you want. You can't live just for money. That's meaningless. You can't live just for pleasure. That's meaningless. You can't live just for yourself. That's meaningless. If you believe in God, there are real-life decisions you have to make. And they're not always convenient.

God should affect your life-style — your habits, your goals, your family. God should affect how you interact with coworkers, how you deal with your boss, what jobs you accept, and even whether or not you cheat on taxes. God should affect your opinions, the candidates you vote for, the policies of the country in which you live. And, lest we forget, the way you treat your opponents.

If you believe in God, He must become the standard by which you evaluate your decisions. Or, to put it more traditionally, God is the Judge.

Our Living God must be a part of living. Integrated into our lives on every level. And either we start to develop this kind of relationship with Him, or, practically speaking, we are functional atheists.

How do you begin? First, choose a God you like.

No one knows what or who God really is, so you might as well pick an image of God you're comfortable with.

We've chosen to describe God as "He." Maybe because we're traditional. Or chauvinistic. Or both. But God could also be a She. Light-skinned. Dark-skinned. Blonde or brunette. Some people think of God as a ghost. Or the "The Force" of Star Wars fame.

The important thing is to begin to relate to God in a way that makes you feel closer emotionally and intellectually. As you get smarter, so will your picture.

Then, it doesn't hurt to strike up a conversation. Most people call that *praying*. It may feel a little dumb at first.

But let's face it, any Intelligent Living Spirit should be able to hear us. And listen to us. Or what good is He?

By praying, we open up a dialogue with God. We get to know each other. And we allow ourselves to listen to God. It's a way of linking our lives with the greater Life Who created us. It's a way of joining purposes in His plan.

But the uses of prayer have been distorted over the years. There is a correct way to pray. And an incorrect way.

It's ridiculous to pray for something that's already happened. Or to try to make something materialize out of nothing. That's asking God to alter the flow of time and change the laws of physics for you. That a sure-fire way to set yourself up for a big disappointment.

It's ridiculous to pray opportunistically. To offer prayer in times of trouble. And abandon it when things are hunky-dory. That's hardly the basis of a close personal relationship.

And of course, it's ridiculous to pray for something that's your responsibility. After all, you're a cocreator.

So what can you pray for? In a word, help. If God can't help you, be of some service, He might as well not exist.

God should be able to help you out. Guide your decisions. Inspire you to make correct choices. God should be able to help you recover from your mistakes. And get back on track. God should be able to give you strength.

God should be able to help "connect" you to life more deeply and more intimately than before. You may be able to feel God's presence in the people and events that enter your life. You may feel an order, a rhythm, a sense of wholeness and integration that makes it seem as if things were being *planned*.

This might not happen immediately, because a relationship with God requires a certain amount of devotion, on both sides, before it begins to happen. It also requires some discipline. God has to become at least as much a part of your daily ritual as brushing your teeth.

Perhaps that's why religions have been so popular. A religion can help you make God personal. It can give you a picture of God if you don't have one of your own. It can give you structure, focus, support from others. It can get you started on prayer. It can help provide a moral framework on which to base your decisions.

But religion is not *the* answer. Only God can be that.

Unlike God, religions are not perfect. They are not eternal. Even the oldest ones, and the most dogmatic ones, change. In a way, they are more like bodies than like spirits. One year you eat fish on Fridays, the next year you don't. Theologies evolve. But slowly. Because they affect millions of lives.

And every religion, to some extent, must be adapted to your particular circumstances. Even the most devout clergyman is not absolved from reconciling religious teachings with his own conscience. It's a continual process. It's called *growing.*

Within the structure of a religion it is easier for people to grow, within themselves and in their relationship to God, if the religion encourages questions. Then, you can work through your difficulties, grapple with your doubts, and gain a closer, more intimate feeling toward God. It's certainly worth a try.

However, sometimes a religion can get in the way of God. And it should never be allowed to do that. Maybe the religion you were born into doesn't work for you. Maybe it's become too associated with guilt or repression, or with your "old self." Maybe it's too structured. Maybe it's not structured enough.

Maybe you need a new religion. A new picture of God. Maybe you need a religion that's more meditative, less moralistic, or more mystical.

On the other hand, there is no rule that says you need a religion at all. If God is the source of everything, it's absurd to think you need to walk any path at all except the path of your own life. That's personal enough.

Few of us can be saints, avatars, or holy messengers. These roles seem reserved for only some very special people. For most of us, and for most of the universe, perfection is not a God-given state, but a process. Nevertheless it's a process we can all begin. We may start out slowly, but we can all begin to participate in God's plan. We can all develop, at our own pace, a personal relationship with God. One that suits our nature. One that makes us feel good about Him. And about ourselves.

When we do, we may discover inside ourselves the source of all religion. It may not be audible at first. But ever so gently, it will make its presence heard.

The Bible calls it the "still small voice" of God. It doesn't get any more personal than that.

Smart Way 7
God Is Real

So now we're hearing voices. Soon we'll be seeing apparitions and defending our sanity.

Is our personal God just a hallucination? a phantasm? Does He join the ranks of elves and gnomes? Of Big Foot and the Loch Ness monster? Is God merely an invention by some highly imaginative creator?

Maybe we all should have stayed sun worshippers and given up an idea as cumbersome as monotheism. Idol worship is easier. At least we could all point to — and see — the great lord sun. At least for half a day, we could all agree he was there. Then again, we could always switch to the moon at night.

Yet if God is *only* personal, there is nothing that separates Him from the visions of witch doctors or madmen. If God is *only* personal, there could be a different God for everyone. Our God would degenerate into a pantheon of demigods, all competing for cosmic supremacy. Welcome back to ancient Canaan!

But our God must be the One God. He cannot just be personal. He must be universal. The God of our inner world and our outer world.

God cannot just be a subjective experience, or He is an illusion.

God must exist objectively, or He has no substance; He can never be considered real.

Though our personalizations may differ, God must have attributes people can agree upon, as readily as they agree that a chair exists, or emotions. The experience of God must be able to be shared, or it cannot be credible.

God must have definite qualities that can be experienced and reexperienced. In a sense, we should be able to apply the scientific method to God. Our experiences, our experiments in His reality, should be able to be repeated, validated, at different times, by different people, by different faiths. That's the only way we can be sure we have a God that's real.

Remarkably, throughout the ages, there has been little debate about the reality of God. Most of the conflict between people, between religions, has been over rituals. Over political differences. Over nuances of theology. People problems. Not God problems.

Many religions have forgotten that their personal picture of God is just a way to feel closer to something impossible to picture. They mistake their image of God for God Himself, and then insist that "their" God is the only God.

In reality, few ministers, rabbis, priests, or saffron-robed Krishnas could seriously debate the sense of wholeness — within themselves, with others, with all of creation — that is the *experience* of God.

Once we dump religious divisiveness in the garbage, where it belongs, we are left with a God that is like Ivory Soap — 99 and 44/100% pure — with qualities people can agree upon. God is not *just* personal, but transpersonal. He does have an objective nature. Our God has a definite, real personality.

For one thing, God is *gracious*. He is a good Host, always ready to invite you in. All you have to do is knock. God is accessible. He is willing to reveal Himself to you. But He only reveals part of His Nature at any one time, to any one person. Only as much as you're capable of handling.

That's why religious revelations generally don't happen en masse, but only to "chosen" persons, who then carry God's message to others. Jesus, Moses, Buddha, all possessed characters that were sufficiently developed spiritually to receive God's revelation.

In general, the more you are open to God, the more He is open to you. The more you keep growing, the closer your relationship with God becomes, and the more you realize that God also possesses another quality: He is *just*.

God reveals Himself to be extraordinarily fair and considerate. His laws, which help guide us in His plan. are demanding. They require tremendous wrestling and heart-searching. Nevertheless, they uphold the dignity of our lives, the purpose of our world. And once again, they are laws that God Himself also obeys. There is no double-dealing. There is a covenant. God doesn't ask anything of us He doesn't ask of Himself.

Also, God is *faithful*. He keeps His promises. His Word is etched in stone, or if you prefer, incarnate in Creation.

Therefore you should not "fear" God in the usual retribu-
tive sense of the word. A faithful God would never lash out
unpredictably, uncontrollably, and smite you unexpectedly
for wrongdoing.

You should fear God for what he exposes within you.
Confronting God, comparing yourself to Him, reveals your
frailties, your false selves, and the gulf, the sins, within
you. God provokes an honesty that is terrifying. Who
among us, in this respect, could be so perfect that he
would not be God-fearing?

But God is also *compassionate*. He feels for us. For
the dichotomies of our lives. He understands the difficulties of correct choice and the potential we all have for evil.

And luckily, He's *forgiving*. God doesn't hold a grudge.
You can't make one mistake and be damned forever. God
could not do that and uphold our free will at the same
time. As creators, we must be allowed to choose freely the
first time, and the second time. Even if we make the same
mistake twice.

But that doesn't mean we are permitted to take advan-
tage of His forgiveness — and once forgiven, we intentional-
ly flub again. That will only separate us from God, and
keep us from experiencing His Personality on a deeper
level. Indeed, it can feel as if God has withdrawn from our
life, that we are being "punished," when in reality, it's we
who have cut ourselves off from God. Because for a personal God to be real, He must be taken seriously.

Fortunately, God is also *patient*. He is always there to
help guide you back home, to redeem you. If you chose to,
you could have all the time in the universe to grow. Or, in
the words of that immortal cocktail lounge song, "If it
takes forever, I will wait for you." Sooner or later God
knows you'll come around. After all, there's no place to

run from Someone Who is everywhere. Except from yourself.

But of all these divine personality traits, there is one that seems to sum them all up.

God is gracious, just, faithful, compassionate, forgiving, and patient because He is *loving*. Or as one great scripture puts it so succinctly: "God Is Love."

My God, what a complicated route we've taken! From the origin of the universe to the end of this lesson. Only to come up with something so simple.

Was it worth the trip?

Smart Way 8
God Is Fulfillment

t's always there, lurking in the shadows. It can slither up to us at any time. Coiling itself around our hearts, paralyzing our minds, it begins to squeeze, ever so gently at first. Then, tighter, and tighter, until it suffocates our faith.

It's not a serpent. But it is a devil. It is *doubt!*

No matter how disarming our playfulness has been, how rationally we present our smart idea of God, doubt is a force to be reckoned with.

If God is so great, why can't He end it? Why can't He heal our disbelief? Banish it to the twilight zone?

But perhaps the question is not whether God can help heal our doubts. The real question may be, *What doubts*?

For our petty intellectual doubts, God can say little.

If we insist that seeing is believing, an invisible God is

worthless. If matter is the only thing we trust as real, Spirit is a fantasy; love, then, is a delusion. If only the quantifiable is credible, an Infinity that is counted as One is absurd.

But there are other kinds of doubts for which a God Who is Love can do a lot.

For one, the kind of doubt that questions if life has meaning . . . the doubt that wonders about permanence in a world that never stops changing . . . the kind of existential doubt that laughs at life's travails but hears the question "Is that all there is?" reverberate, like a tinman's chest without a heart.

For this kind of doubt, significant doubt, meaningful doubt, nobody has ever found a better solution than God.

God gives us the definitive answer to the questions "Where do we come from?" and "Where are we going?" He says we are not an accident, but a planned birth. We have a spiritual Parent of Pure Love Who existed before existence.

But He says He isn't the only one who is Love. We are love, too, although we are not fully aware of it. Because we are spiritually immature, a little stupid, if you will.

Nevertheless, God says we are growing smarter. Toward greater awareness of the perfect love, inside us and outside us. We are growing, whether we like it or not, whether we aid our progress or hinder it. It's His plan.

So God says, despite its appearance, Creation isn't chaotic. It has order. Everything is just a different aspect of a single force, a unified field of Divine Love.

This Love does not teeter-totter with indecision. It is absolute. Unwavering. Perfect. So perfect it can even feel compassion for hatred.

God eliminates our doubt about life. He says life does indeed have meaning and purpose. But unlike Darwin, God says that purpose is not just survival. Life evolves solely (soul-ly?) for spiritual perfection. Organic structures become more complex, bodies evolve, to help facilitate this goal. The more advanced a species, the more its consciousness resembles the creativity and intelligence of the Creator. In short, man apes God.

God ends our moral doubts. Right and wrong, good and bad, are not just relative concepts. There is an absolute gold standard of morality by which everything can be judged: God Himself. Infinite, Unchanging Love.

God dispels our philosophical doubts. He says that "more exists than meets the eye," that there is a reality that transcends but includes the reality of our senses. A more fundamental reality that is by nature Good. Guess Who?

Although we can't know Him completely, God says if we love Him with all our heart, all our mind, all our strength, if we love our neighbor as ourselves, we can get pretty damn close.

God removes our social doubts. He says society's main purpose is to encourage spiritual freedom; economic freedom by itself is meaningless. A full belly is the first step to filling the soul. That's why He encourages charity. Not a welfare system that demeans the person it serves. But a charity that raises the dignity of people, like providing jobs.

God explodes our political doubts. He says any relationship with Him must be sought freely. Any government that interferes with that freedom is immoral, because it defies our living covenant with Him as cocreators of the world.

But unlike General God, our God says absolutely, positively, under no circumstances, do the ends justify the means. No matter how noble the idea, it is immoral to force someone to conform to it. Promoting morality with a pistol is not God's way. There is a big difference spiritually between persuasion and coercion.

God shatters our doubts about the value of religion. Religious divisiveness is not loving and is therefore not from God. Any religion that does not allow for freedom of conscience is as sinful as any totalitarian government. The religion that is incapable of respecting someone else's truth can never claim to be itself "true."

God heals our psychological doubt. He says, "Buck up. No matter how hard life is, you're not alone. There are no cosmic orphans." He is always there to help, guide, and redeem us. He offers free lifetime membership to His spiritual health club for anyone who wants it, without restrictions. The only thing we need to do is stop being so obsessed with ourselves, and look to Him.

God says sin isn't necessary. He offers us a very precious alternative: hope. A way to close the gulf within us and seal it. Our thoughts and actions don't have to squabble. Who we are, and who we can be, are one and the same. If we love Him, love others, and love ourselves.

That's the best psychotherapy we could ever have. Better than Freud. Better than Jung. Better than EST. And a lot cheaper.

Self-love! What a great idea! But God reminds us it's nothing new. Love is our original nature. We weren't born guilt-ridden. There's no more "positive transference" than that.

And when God is through saying everything He can about our doubts, we're not just left with a feeling of love, but also something else — the one thing human beings seem to live for, drive for, strive for, more than anything

More than food. More than sex. More than God.

Ironically, it's as elusive as God. No one can prove it exists. But few of us ever doubt its possibility.

Ah yes, if only we could believe in God, as much as we believe in this thing called *happiness*.

Perhaps they're one and the same?

Smart Way 9
God Is Forever

"Gentlemen, and of course ladies, after putting you through this lengthy presentation, we are proud to announce that we have found the slogan for the God account. We're ready to roll out the campaign immediately. Launch internationally, interpersonally, and if need be, interdimensionally. We are going to blitz the ether with it.

"Ready for this: 'Get Happy. Get God.' O.K., so it's not as catchy as 'Where's the beef?' or 'See the U.S.A. in a Chevrolet'. But you gotta admit, it really says it."

The promise of fulfillment can sound more like sales hype than truth. Especially when confronted with the most devastating doubt of all — how appropriate that we've saved it for last. Because it is a most final doubt: Death.

The Masked Executioner always seems to stand one step behind us, scimitar in hand. In one fell swoop, He mocks our faith and delivers a coupe de grâce to our smart way of thinking about God. Not to mention all our activities.

Death scorns us. It reminds us all too painfully that we are, in part, matter. It forces us to admit we are perishable. And even the promise of an Eternal God can seem like so much snake oil when face-to-face with the power of death.

Death has this way of making everything, including God, seem futile. Death can take most everything we've worked for, struggled for, and bring it to a grinding halt.

It is often our attitude toward death, even more than toward life, that determines how we live. Some people race around like madmen, trying to get it all in — the Rolling Stone philosophy. Cramming their lives with one thrill after another, they race through life trying to beat death at its own game. Alas, isn't there a little stone rolling in all of us?

But whether you run toward death, or walk, sooner or later everyone gets there. And few people, atheist or theist, when in death's embrace, can avoid a self-reflection. No one can help but mull over their accomplishments, good, bad, or indifferent, and wonder if they actually achieved anything at all.

For many, it may be the first time they have stopped long enough to think about how they have lived their lives. And it is no coincidence that it is the first time many people think seriously about God. Often, they've ignored God until the final hour, when, so commonly, they reach out in hope that the stupid way of thinking they were raised with has a shred of truth. They call a priest for the first time in years to administer last rites. They grope into their fading minds to recall the obscure words "Shema Yisroel."

But who can blame anyone. Death is the great unknown. Death appears so opposite from the idea of everlasting life that it has frequently been turned into God's rival instead of God's Hand. A demigod, complete with its own independent mythology.

Yet to death, however powerful it appears, God lifts the Executioner's mask. Firmly and deliberately, He sticks out His tongue and says, "Phooey."

God says we are immortal, because we were created from His immortal Spirit. That is our true nature. And though we may not have been aware of it, we have always been immortal.

Eternal life will not be "added" by God to our lives. Eternal life *is* our gift of life, though we may still be a little too stupid to appreciate it. Although we are making a passageway between two realities, and it can seem dark, God tells us we will not at all cease to be. We will not fade to black like the end of a movie.

On the contrary, God says our consciousness lives on. It will retain its integrity through the passage of death. And we will continue our purpose in life. We will continue to grow spiritually toward greater perfection and love.

Some believe this requires a cleansing period, a purgatory. But it may not necessarily be some flaming hell. It can just be a blazing fire of introspection. A self-critical honesty that burns in our consciousness.

Others believe that there are other mortal lifetimes, other bodies, other opportunities for continuing our spiritual growth. We get a chance, they say, to do it all over again, until we get it right. Around and around and around we go, where it stops, only God knows.

Still others speak of resurrection into a new and different kind of body. A spiritual body, which enters some alternate reality of pure Goodness that we call Heaven.

Advances in medical technology have enabled medical

professionals to "pull patients back" to life. Patients talk of seeing and feeling a warm, glowing, loving, white light reaching out to them. They identify this light with God Himself. Even patients whose only religious experience has been disbelief have shared this experience.

Certainly, the similarity between these now common experiences and the spiritual illuminations of monks and mystics gives us ground to speculate. Is death just a branch of depth psychology? Is it just another aspect of human consciousness?

We can debate the afterlife experience all we want and never really know what happens. Reincarnation, resurrection, or all the heavens and hells of our own imagination are but personal images that affirm one essential truth: God is Forever.

Death is not at all final. If we think it is, that is just incomplete knowledge on our part, just like any doubt.

The real issue is not death at all, nor past lives, nor future lives, but how we live this life. It is only our worldly accomplishments that really die. The homes. The cars. The bankbooks. The power trips. The self-importance. All our false gods. And false selves. "You can't take it with you," as they say.

But that's not true of our spiritual accomplishments. Acts of kindness, charity, and love live on. Within us. And in the lives we've touched. Long after we pass on.

There need be no deathbed of moral remorse or missed opportunity to a person who has lived life in a personal relationship with God, expanding and growing in love of Him, love of neighbor, love of self. To one for whom God has become real, the passage through death need not be terrifying or empty. It can simply feel like a continuation. Just one more step in becoming smarter, in experiencing the wholeness of Divine Love.

To this person, any victory death has is at best temporary, dwarfed by the overpowering promise of Eternal Life.

If this sounds like a sell-line, it's persuasive.

What more beautiful way for a life to draw to a close.

Smart Way 10
God Is All

I f this *Beginning* Who is *Living*, Who is the *Creator*, and the *Creator of Creators*, Who has a *Plan*, is both *Personal* and *Real*, Who brings *Fulfillment*, and Who is *Forever* still sounds a bit complicated, let's simplify it. With the biggest, littlest word of all: *All*.

God is All. That's All there is. There's nothing else. God is It. The Total. The Big Sum. Or, if you want to get fancy, the Infinite Monad, as one philosopher dubbed Him.

God is All. How's that for simplification! But, wrap your head around "All," and you might want to go back to chopping God into pieces. After all, little pieces are a helluva lot easier to digest.

Because *All* means just that: All. It means there is nothing that could be or exist without God. It means that all time, all space, all laws of nature, all natural phenomena, all physiological activities, all psychological phenomena, all societies, all politics, all relationships, all thoughts, all emotions, all life, all non-life — they're all-included in this All.

Indeed, there are so many aspects to God, we seem to have complicated matters even more. We seem to have obliterated the distinction between God and Creation completely — not an uncommon problem among theologians.

However, there is one other three-letter word that goes hand in hand with *All*, which can keep us from spreading God so thin we dissolve Him into pantheism. Turn Him into Mom Nature. That word is *One*.

God is One. *Singular. Solo. Unique.* God is the one ground for everything there is, and the one purpose. This is the understanding that the ancient Hebrews brought the world: *God is One.* And it became the foundation of Judaism, Christianity, and Islam.

Reality may appear diverse, even disparate. But in reality, it is all part of this one singular force, this One Consciousness that we call God.

God's Consciousness manifests differently at different points on the evolutionary scale. Rocks appear unconscious, because they are stuck on the bottom. Plants appear more conscious, because they are higher up. Animals begin to manifest the rudiments of true consciousness. And humans, at least at the present time, seem the ultimate terrestrial standard — once again, they're self-conscious, like God Himself. And can choose to participate in God's creative work.

All creation seems part of one huge consciousness pecking order, beginning from and growing toward that One-Consciousness–of-All, God. All life seems to grow physically, mentally, and spiritually in increasing complexity, reflecting more and more the singularly complex Nature of its Creator.

And not surprisingly, this seems no less true for the creations of God's cocreator, us.

As all our scientific knowledge grows more complex, it reveals more and more of that One Intelligence.

As all our philosophical truths grow more and more sublime, they reveal more and more of that One Truth.

As all our moral actions grow wiser and wiser, they reveal more and more of that One Wisdom.

As we all treat each other more lovingly, we reveal more and more of that One Love that created us.

As neighbor joins neighbor, we all grow toward oneness. As nation joins nation, we all grow toward becoming one mankind.

And just as we evolve spiritually, just as we grow in oneness through history, so should all our knowledge grow in oneness, until we no longer have any doubts whatsoever.

If there is One Truth, then science and religion, once one discipline prior to the so-called "Age of Enlightenment," must eventually grow toward oneness again — joined by psychology, sociology, political science, biology, chemistry, physics, and the pantheon of academic demigods mankind presently worships.

One by one, all our disciplines, all our fragmented knowledge, all our partial truths, incomplete ideas, and stupid ways may grow toward completeness, fuse into one; creating the ultimate smart way to think about God. One understanding of our inner world. One understanding of our outer world. One understanding of the one creation, born of the One Creator.

Indeed, such new disciplines as psychopharmacology, sociobiology, and neurolinguistic programming only serve to show how artificial have been our categories of knowledge until now. We're building bridges over illusory separations. Pretty stupid, huh? But getting smarter.

Yes, if God is the "All that is One," then Creation is the "all that is *becoming* One." Whether God-made or man-made, all creation is part of one simple, but mammoth Spiritual Recycling Center, which is no less than the Essence of God Himself. All the pieces fit together like a puzzle, because they came from One Puzzle: the mystery of God.

By working to create oneness in all we think, in all we feel, in all we do, by fusing all we are into one, and linking in oneness with all others, with all life, with all creation, we are simply mirroring the One Spirit of All: God. This is what the Messianic Age, of which so many religions speak, is all about.

All for One. And One for All. That's one cheer that should inspire team spirit in us all.

Epilogue:
The Adventure
Begins

Well, Sunday school is over. And our smart ways of thinking about God have apparently come to an end. But only apparently, because with God, there is no end.

There's only Unchanging, Eternal Truth. There's only Pure, Infinite Consciousness. There's only an Ever-living Spirit of Perfect Love.

The end? It's really no different from the beginning, because ultimately, all differences, all our mortal distinctions, dissolve before the Oneness and Completeness of God.

In the end, there is only one reality: "I am that I am." The reality of God.

As for us, here and now, reality is not quite so simple. God *is*, but we are *becoming*.

Like the entire universe in which we live, we are growing, maturing, evolving, and participating in the never-end-

113

ing process of perfection — a process that leads us, every moment, one step closer to full awareness of the Divine Nature.

One day we will get there, perhaps. But until then, all we can have is faith. There is no proof we can offer about God, except the journey itself.

It's a journey we all have to make. Each of us in his own way. And although there may be others to lend a helping hand, ultimately we all have to find our own beliefs, our own smart way to think about God.

That's not always easy. The path is frequently paved in doubt and fear. And even the most faithful cannot avoid a stumble or two.

So, by way of a summary, we'd like to leave you with six simple rules, a few signposts to help guide you on your way.

You have a smart way of thinking about God **IF** it

- Opens you up to the experience of God. An experience that must be lived, shared, and felt.
- Makes God, not man, the standard for everything.
- Allows you to be fully human — mind, heart, and body.
- Helps you feel more whole, within yourself, and with others. And allows others the same opportunity.
- Can be personalized.
- Can grow as you grow and continually reveal more of the Truth.

These rules aren't infallible. But they can help you identify holes in the way you do think. They can help make you aware of difficulties you may be having, or may have in the future, and point to a direction in which you need to grow.

But the important thing is — whatever the difficulties — keep working at it. Because if you don't, that's when problems begin to set in. That's when doubts can become so overwhelming they erode the ground you stand on. That's when you can start to follow a belief blindly — going through the motions with emptiness in your heart. That's when you can start feeling abandoned by God. Or worse, start to abandon God.

To try is holy! It's remarkable how, with a little persistence, with a little help from others, you can get through your trials, your "faith crisis," and find the light at the end of the tunnel.

Doubts are always healthy when they inspire us to persevere and to grow beyond them. Doubts are crippling only when we refuse to face the challenge they present to us.

Everyone has doubts. And why not? Shouldn't we always question whether or not what we believe — about God, or about anything else — is true? Shouldn't we always try to deepen our understanding and make our beliefs more meaningful?

To grow, or not to grow? That is the real question. And when you think about it, despite our God-given free will, we have — ironically — only one choice.

Whether we admit it or not, we have already taken a leap of faith the moment we're born. Every day we face the world, with all its uncertainties, hoping to find one thing— something, anything — certain.

So, in a way, thinking about God is really no different from living life. We have no choice but to start out where we are, face forward, and take the next step. We have no choice but to grow smarter.

That's what the adventure of God, and life, is all about. It's the adventure of searching for meaning, for purpose, for happiness, never stopping.

To live any other way would just not be very smart.

About the Authors

MICHAEL SHEVACK is an advertising executive and award-winning copywriter whose clients have included Apple Computer, Gillette, Lever, Colgate-Palmolive, among others. He has recently turned his writing talents to religious and spiritual matters, his articles having appeared in numerous publications. He lives in Bucks County, Pennsylvania, with his wife Trish and three children.

JACK BEMPORAD, an ordained rabbi since 1959, was a Fulbright Scholar at the University of Rome and holds an honorary Doctorate of Divinity from Hebrew Union College. He is a world-renowned leader in interfaith dialogue and has led Christian-Jewish missions throughout Europe. He is presently director of the Center for Christian-Jewish Understanding at Sacred Heart University in Connecticut and senior rabbinic scholar at Chavurah Bet Shalom in New Jersey, where he lives with his wife Alex. He has edited and written numerous articles and books.